My BUCKET LIST

01

I WANT TO DO THIS BECAUSE _____

_____

TO MAKE THIS HAPPEN I NEED TO_____

_____

_____ *Let's do this* _____

DATE COMPLETED _____ LOCATION _____

SOLO / WITH _____

THE STORY_____

_____

_____

_____

_____

_____

_____

THE BEST PART_____

_____

_____

WHAT I LEARNED_____

_____

_____

02

_____

_____

I WANT TO DO THIS BECAUSE _____

_____

TO MAKE THIS HAPPEN I NEED TO _____

_____

_____ *Let's do this* _____

DATE COMPLETED _____ LOCATION _____

SOLO / WITH _____

THE STORY _____

_____

_____

_____

_____

_____

THE BEST PART _____

_____

_____

WHAT I LEARNED _____

_____

_____

03 _____

_____

I WANT TO DO THIS BECAUSE _____

_____

TO MAKE THIS HAPPEN I NEED TO _____

_____

_____ *Let's do this* _____

DATE COMPLETED _____ LOCATION _____

SOLO / WITH _____

THE STORY _____

_____

_____

_____

_____

_____

THE BEST PART _____

_____

_____

WHAT I LEARNED _____

_____

_____

_____

_____ ***04***
_____

I WANT TO DO THIS BECAUSE _____
_____

TO MAKE THIS HAPPEN I NEED TO_____
_____

_____ *Let's do this* _____

DATE COMPLETED _____ LOCATION _____
SOLO / WITH _____
THE STORY_____
_____
_____
_____
_____
_____
_____

THE BEST PART_____
_____
_____

WHAT I LEARNED_____
_____
_____

05 _____

_____

I WANT TO DO THIS BECAUSE _____

_____

TO MAKE THIS HAPPEN I NEED TO _____

_____

_____ *Let's do this* _____

DATE COMPLETED _____ LOCATION _____

SOLO / WITH _____

THE STORY _____

_____

_____

_____

_____

_____

_____

THE BEST PART _____

_____

_____

WHAT I LEARNED _____

_____

_____

06

_____

_____

I WANT TO DO THIS BECAUSE _____

_____

TO MAKE THIS HAPPEN I NEED TO _____

_____

_____ *Let's do this* _____

DATE COMPLETED _____ LOCATION _____

SOLO / WITH _____

THE STORY _____

_____

_____

_____

_____

_____

_____

THE BEST PART _____

_____

_____

WHAT I LEARNED _____

_____

_____

07 _____
_____

I WANT TO DO THIS BECAUSE _____
_____

TO MAKE THIS HAPPEN I NEED TO_____
_____

_____ *Let's do this* _____

DATE COMPLETED _____ LOCATION _____
SOLO / WITH _____
THE STORY_____
_____
_____
_____
_____
_____
_____

THE BEST PART_____
_____
_____

WHAT I LEARNED_____
_____
_____
_____

08

_____

_____

I WANT TO DO THIS BECAUSE _____
_____

TO MAKE THIS HAPPEN I NEED TO _____
_____

_____ *Let's do this* _____

DATE COMPLETED _____ LOCATION _____
SOLO / WITH _____
THE STORY _____
_____
_____
_____
_____
_____
_____

THE BEST PART _____
_____
_____
_____

WHAT I LEARNED _____
_____
_____
_____

09 _____
_____

I WANT TO DO THIS BECAUSE _____
_____

TO MAKE THIS HAPPEN I NEED TO_____
_____

_____ *Let's do this* _____

DATE COMPLETED _____ LOCATION _____
SOLO / WITH _____
THE STORY_____
_____
_____
_____
_____
_____

THE BEST PART_____
_____
_____

WHAT I LEARNED_____
_____
_____

_____

10

_____

I WANT TO DO THIS BECAUSE _____
_____

TO MAKE THIS HAPPEN I NEED TO _____
_____

_____ *Let's do this* _____

DATE COMPLETED _____ LOCATION _____
SOLO / WITH _____
THE STORY _____
_____
_____
_____
_____
_____

THE BEST PART _____
_____
_____

WHAT I LEARNED _____
_____
_____

11 _____

_____

I WANT TO DO THIS BECAUSE _____

_____

TO MAKE THIS HAPPEN I NEED TO _____

_____

_____ *Let's do this* _____

DATE COMPLETED _____ LOCATION _____

SOLO / WITH _____

THE STORY _____

_____

_____

_____

_____

_____

_____

THE BEST PART _____

_____

_____

_____

WHAT I LEARNED _____

_____

_____

12

I WANT TO DO THIS BECAUSE _____
_____

TO MAKE THIS HAPPEN I NEED TO _____
_____

_____ *Let's do this* _____

DATE COMPLETED _____ LOCATION _____
SOLO / WITH _____
THE STORY _____
_____
_____
_____
_____
_____
_____

THE BEST PART _____
_____
_____
_____

WHAT I LEARNED _____
_____
_____
_____

13 _____
_____

I WANT TO DO THIS BECAUSE _____
_____

TO MAKE THIS HAPPEN I NEED TO _____
_____

_____ Let's do this _____

DATE COMPLETED _____ LOCATION _____
SOLO / WITH _____
THE STORY _____
_____
_____
_____
_____
_____

THE BEST PART _____
_____
_____

WHAT I LEARNED _____
_____
_____
_____

14

_____
_____

I WANT TO DO THIS BECAUSE _____
_____

TO MAKE THIS HAPPEN I NEED TO _____
_____

_____ _Let's do this_ _____

DATE COMPLETED _____ LOCATION _____
SOLO / WITH _____
THE STORY _____
_____
_____
_____
_____
_____
_____

THE BEST PART _____
_____
_____

WHAT I LEARNED _____
_____
_____

15 _____
_____

I WANT TO DO THIS BECAUSE _____
_____

TO MAKE THIS HAPPEN I NEED TO _____
_____

_____ *Let's do this* _____

DATE COMPLETED _____ LOCATION _____
SOLO / WITH _____
THE STORY _____
_____
_____
_____
_____
_____
_____

THE BEST PART _____
_____
_____

WHAT I LEARNED _____
_____
_____

_____ **16**
_____

I WANT TO DO THIS BECAUSE _____
_____

TO MAKE THIS HAPPEN I NEED TO _____
_____

_____ *Let's do this* _____

DATE COMPLETED _____ LOCATION _____
SOLO / WITH _____
THE STORY_____
_____
_____
_____
_____
_____

THE BEST PART_____
_____
_____

WHAT I LEARNED_____
_____
_____
_____

17 _____
_____

I WANT TO DO THIS BECAUSE _____
_____

TO MAKE THIS HAPPEN I NEED TO_____
_____

_____ *Let's do this* _____

DATE COMPLETED _____ LOCATION _____
SOLO / WITH _____
THE STORY_____
_____
_____
_____
_____
_____

THE BEST PART_____
_____
_____

WHAT I LEARNED_____
_____
_____

18

_____

_____

I WANT TO DO THIS BECAUSE _____

_____

TO MAKE THIS HAPPEN I NEED TO_____

_____

_____ *Let's do this* _____

DATE COMPLETED _____ LOCATION _____

SOLO / WITH _____

THE STORY_____

_____

_____

_____

_____

_____

THE BEST PART_____

_____

_____

WHAT I LEARNED_____

_____

_____

_____

19 _____
_____

I WANT TO DO THIS BECAUSE _____
_____

TO MAKE THIS HAPPEN I NEED TO _____
_____

_____ *Let's do this* _____

DATE COMPLETED _____ LOCATION _____
SOLO / WITH _____
THE STORY _____
_____
_____
_____
_____
_____
_____

THE BEST PART _____
_____
_____

WHAT I LEARNED _____
_____
_____

20

_____
_____

I WANT TO DO THIS BECAUSE _____
_____

TO MAKE THIS HAPPEN I NEED TO _____
_____

_____ *Let's do this* _____

DATE COMPLETED _____ LOCATION _____

SOLO / WITH _____

THE STORY _____
_____
_____
_____
_____
_____
_____

THE BEST PART _____
_____
_____
_____

WHAT I LEARNED _____
_____
_____

21 _____
_____

I WANT TO DO THIS BECAUSE _____
_____

TO MAKE THIS HAPPEN I NEED TO _____
_____

_____ Let's do this _____

DATE COMPLETED _____ LOCATION _____
SOLO / WITH _____
THE STORY _____
_____
_____
_____
_____
_____
_____

THE BEST PART _____
_____
_____
_____

WHAT I LEARNED _____
_____
_____
_____

22

I WANT TO DO THIS BECAUSE _____

_____

TO MAKE THIS HAPPEN I NEED TO_____

_____

_____ *Let's do this* _____

DATE COMPLETED _____ LOCATION _____

SOLO / WITH _____

THE STORY_____

_____

_____

_____

_____

_____

THE BEST PART_____

_____

_____

WHAT I LEARNED_____

_____

_____

23 _____

_____

I WANT TO DO THIS BECAUSE _____

_____

TO MAKE THIS HAPPEN I NEED TO _____

_____

_____ *Let's do this* _____

DATE COMPLETED _____ LOCATION _____

SOLO / WITH _____

THE STORY _____

_____

_____

_____

_____

_____

_____

THE BEST PART _____

_____

_____

WHAT I LEARNED _____

_____

_____

24

_____

_____

I WANT TO DO THIS BECAUSE _____

_____

TO MAKE THIS HAPPEN I NEED TO_____

_____

_____ *Let's do this* _____

DATE COMPLETED _____ LOCATION _____

SOLO / WITH _____

THE STORY_____

_____

_____

_____

_____

_____

_____

THE BEST PART_____

_____

_____

WHAT I LEARNED_____

_____

_____

_____

25 _____
_____

I WANT TO DO THIS BECAUSE _____
_____

TO MAKE THIS HAPPEN I NEED TO_____
_____

_____ Let's do this _____

DATE COMPLETED _____ LOCATION _____
SOLO / WITH _____
THE STORY_____
_____
_____
_____
_____
_____
_____

THE BEST PART_____
_____
_____
_____

WHAT I LEARNED_____
_____
_____
_____

26

I WANT TO DO THIS BECAUSE _____
_____

TO MAKE THIS HAPPEN I NEED TO _____
_____

_____ *Let's do this* _____

DATE COMPLETED _____ LOCATION _____
SOLO / WITH _____
THE STORY _____
_____
_____
_____
_____
_____
_____

THE BEST PART _____
_____
_____

WHAT I LEARNED _____
_____
_____
_____

27 _____

_____

I WANT TO DO THIS BECAUSE _____

_____

TO MAKE THIS HAPPEN I NEED TO _____

_____

_____ Let's do this _____

DATE COMPLETED _____ LOCATION _____

SOLO / WITH _____

THE STORY_____

_____

_____

_____

_____

_____

THE BEST PART_____

_____

_____

WHAT I LEARNED_____

_____

_____

28

_____

_____

I WANT TO DO THIS BECAUSE _____

_____

TO MAKE THIS HAPPEN I NEED TO _____

_____

_____ *Let's do this* _____

DATE COMPLETED _____ LOCATION _____

SOLO / WITH _____

THE STORY _____

_____

_____

_____

_____

_____

THE BEST PART _____

_____

_____

WHAT I LEARNED _____

_____

_____

_____

29 _____
_____

I WANT TO DO THIS BECAUSE _____
_____

TO MAKE THIS HAPPEN I NEED TO _____
_____

_____ Let's do this _____

DATE COMPLETED _____ LOCATION _____
SOLO / WITH _____
THE STORY _____
_____
_____
_____
_____
_____

THE BEST PART _____
_____
_____

WHAT I LEARNED _____
_____
_____

30

_____

_____

I WANT TO DO THIS BECAUSE _____

_____

TO MAKE THIS HAPPEN I NEED TO _____

_____

_____ *Let's do this* _____

DATE COMPLETED _____ LOCATION _____

SOLO / WITH _____

THE STORY _____

_____

_____

_____

_____

_____

THE BEST PART _____

_____

_____

WHAT I LEARNED _____

_____

_____

31 _____
_____

I WANT TO DO THIS BECAUSE _____
_____

TO MAKE THIS HAPPEN I NEED TO _____
_____

_____ *Let's do this* _____

DATE COMPLETED _____ LOCATION _____
SOLO / WITH _____
THE STORY _____
_____
_____
_____
_____
_____
_____

THE BEST PART _____
_____
_____
_____

WHAT I LEARNED _____
_____
_____

32

I WANT TO DO THIS BECAUSE _____

_____

TO MAKE THIS HAPPEN I NEED TO _____

_____

_____ *Let's do this* _____

DATE COMPLETED _____ LOCATION _____

SOLO / WITH _____

THE STORY _____

_____

_____

_____

_____

_____

THE BEST PART _____

_____

_____

WHAT I LEARNED _____

_____

_____

_____

33 _____
_____

I WANT TO DO THIS BECAUSE _____
_____

TO MAKE THIS HAPPEN I NEED TO _____
_____

_____ *Let's do this* _____

DATE COMPLETED _____ LOCATION _____
SOLO / WITH _____
THE STORY _____
_____
_____
_____
_____
_____
_____

THE BEST PART _____
_____
_____

WHAT I LEARNED _____
_____
_____

34

I WANT TO DO THIS BECAUSE _____
_____

TO MAKE THIS HAPPEN I NEED TO _____
_____

_____ *Let's do this* _____

DATE COMPLETED _____ LOCATION _____
SOLO / WITH _____
THE STORY _____
_____
_____
_____
_____
_____
_____

THE BEST PART _____
_____
_____

WHAT I LEARNED _____
_____
_____
_____

35 _____
_____

I WANT TO DO THIS BECAUSE _____
_____

TO MAKE THIS HAPPEN I NEED TO _____
_____

_____ *Let's do this* _____

DATE COMPLETED _____ LOCATION _____
SOLO / WITH _____
THE STORY _____
_____
_____
_____
_____
_____
_____

THE BEST PART _____
_____
_____
_____

WHAT I LEARNED _____
_____
_____
_____

36

_____

_____

I WANT TO DO THIS BECAUSE _____
_____

TO MAKE THIS HAPPEN I NEED TO _____
_____

_____ *Let's do this* _____

DATE COMPLETED _____ LOCATION _____
SOLO / WITH _____
THE STORY _____
_____
_____
_____
_____
_____
_____

THE BEST PART _____
_____
_____

WHAT I LEARNED _____
_____
_____

37 _____
_____

I WANT TO DO THIS BECAUSE _____
_____

TO MAKE THIS HAPPEN I NEED TO _____
_____

_____ *Let's do this* _____

DATE COMPLETED _____ LOCATION _____
SOLO / WITH _____
THE STORY _____
_____
_____
_____
_____
_____
_____

THE BEST PART _____
_____
_____

WHAT I LEARNED _____
_____
_____

38

_____
_____

I WANT TO DO THIS BECAUSE _____
_____

TO MAKE THIS HAPPEN I NEED TO _____
_____

_____ _Let's do this_ _____

DATE COMPLETED _____ LOCATION _____
SOLO / WITH _____
THE STORY _____
_____
_____
_____
_____
_____
_____

THE BEST PART _____
_____
_____
_____

WHAT I LEARNED _____
_____
_____
_____

39 _____
_____

I WANT TO DO THIS BECAUSE _____
_____

TO MAKE THIS HAPPEN I NEED TO _____
_____

_____ *Let's do this* _____

DATE COMPLETED _____ LOCATION _____
SOLO / WITH _____
THE STORY_____
_____
_____
_____
_____
_____
_____

THE BEST PART_____
_____
_____

WHAT I LEARNED_____
_____
_____

40

_____

_____

I WANT TO DO THIS BECAUSE _____

_____

TO MAKE THIS HAPPEN I NEED TO _____

_____

_____ *Let's do this* _____

DATE COMPLETED _____ LOCATION _____

SOLO / WITH _____

THE STORY_____

_____

_____

_____

_____

_____

_____

THE BEST PART_____

_____

_____

WHAT I LEARNED_____

_____

_____

_____

41 _____
_____

I WANT TO DO THIS BECAUSE _____
_____

TO MAKE THIS HAPPEN I NEED TO _____
_____

_____ Let's do this _____

DATE COMPLETED _____ LOCATION _____

SOLO / WITH _____

THE STORY _____
_____
_____
_____
_____
_____

THE BEST PART _____
_____
_____

WHAT I LEARNED _____
_____
_____
_____

42

_____

I WANT TO DO THIS BECAUSE _____

TO MAKE THIS HAPPEN I NEED TO_____

_____ *Let's do this* _____

DATE COMPLETED _____ LOCATION _____
SOLO / WITH _____
THE STORY_____

THE BEST PART_____

WHAT I LEARNED_____

43 _____
_____

I WANT TO DO THIS BECAUSE _____

_____

TO MAKE THIS HAPPEN I NEED TO _____

_____

_____ *Let's do this* _____

DATE COMPLETED _____ LOCATION _____

SOLO / WITH _____

THE STORY _____

_____

_____

_____

_____

_____

_____

THE BEST PART _____

_____

_____

WHAT I LEARNED _____

_____

_____

_____

44

I WANT TO DO THIS BECAUSE _____

_____

TO MAKE THIS HAPPEN I NEED TO _____

_____

_____ *Let's do this* _____

DATE COMPLETED _____ LOCATION _____

SOLO / WITH _____

THE STORY _____

_____

_____

_____

_____

_____

THE BEST PART _____

_____

_____

WHAT I LEARNED _____

_____

_____

_____

45 _____
_____

I WANT TO DO THIS BECAUSE _____
_____

TO MAKE THIS HAPPEN I NEED TO_____
_____

_____ Let's do this _____

DATE COMPLETED _____ LOCATION _____
SOLO / WITH _____
THE STORY_____
_____
_____
_____
_____
_____
_____

THE BEST PART_____
_____
_____
_____

WHAT I LEARNED_____
_____
_____
_____

46

I WANT TO DO THIS BECAUSE _____

_____

TO MAKE THIS HAPPEN I NEED TO _____

_____

_____ *Let's do this* _____

DATE COMPLETED _____ LOCATION _____

SOLO / WITH _____

THE STORY _____

_____

_____

_____

_____

_____

_____

THE BEST PART _____

_____

_____

WHAT I LEARNED _____

_____

_____

_____

47 _____
_____

I WANT TO DO THIS BECAUSE _____
_____

TO MAKE THIS HAPPEN I NEED TO_____
_____

_____ *Let's do this* _____

DATE COMPLETED _____ LOCATION _____
SOLO / WITH _____
THE STORY_____
_____
_____
_____
_____
_____
_____

THE BEST PART_____
_____
_____

WHAT I LEARNED_____
_____
_____

_____ **48**
_____

I WANT TO DO THIS BECAUSE _____
_____

TO MAKE THIS HAPPEN I NEED TO _____
_____

_____ *Let's do this* _____

DATE COMPLETED _____ LOCATION _____
SOLO / WITH _____
THE STORY _____
_____
_____
_____
_____
_____
_____

THE BEST PART _____
_____
_____

WHAT I LEARNED _____
_____
_____
_____

49 _____
_____

I WANT TO DO THIS BECAUSE _____
_____

TO MAKE THIS HAPPEN I NEED TO_____
_____

_____ *Let's do this* _____

DATE COMPLETED _____ LOCATION _____
SOLO / WITH _____
THE STORY_____
_____
_____
_____
_____
_____
_____

THE BEST PART_____
_____
_____
_____

WHAT I LEARNED_____
_____
_____
_____

50

_____

_____

I WANT TO DO THIS BECAUSE _____

_____

TO MAKE THIS HAPPEN I NEED TO _____

_____

_____ _Let's do this_ _____

DATE COMPLETED _____ LOCATION _____
SOLO / WITH _____
THE STORY _____

_____

_____

_____

_____

_____

THE BEST PART _____

_____

_____

WHAT I LEARNED _____

_____

_____

_____

51

I WANT TO DO THIS BECAUSE _____

_____

TO MAKE THIS HAPPEN I NEED TO_____

_____

_____ *Let's do this* _____

DATE COMPLETED _____ LOCATION _____

SOLO / WITH _____

THE STORY_____

_____

_____

_____

_____

_____

_____

THE BEST PART_____

_____

_____

WHAT I LEARNED_____

_____

_____

52

I WANT TO DO THIS BECAUSE _____

_____

TO MAKE THIS HAPPEN I NEED TO _____

_____

_____ *Let's do this* _____

DATE COMPLETED _____ LOCATION _____
SOLO / WITH _____
THE STORY _____

_____

_____

_____

_____

_____

_____

THE BEST PART _____

_____

_____

WHAT I LEARNED _____

_____

_____

53

I WANT TO DO THIS BECAUSE _____
_____

TO MAKE THIS HAPPEN I NEED TO _____
_____

_____ *Let's do this* _____

DATE COMPLETED _____ LOCATION _____
SOLO / WITH _____
THE STORY _____
_____
_____
_____
_____
_____
_____

THE BEST PART _____
_____
_____

WHAT I LEARNED _____
_____
_____
_____

54

I WANT TO DO THIS BECAUSE _____

_____

TO MAKE THIS HAPPEN I NEED TO _____

_____

_____ *Let's do this* _____

DATE COMPLETED _____ LOCATION _____

SOLO / WITH _____

THE STORY_____

_____

_____

_____

_____

_____

_____

THE BEST PART_____

_____

_____

WHAT I LEARNED_____

_____

_____

55 _____

I WANT TO DO THIS BECAUSE _____
_____

TO MAKE THIS HAPPEN I NEED TO _____
_____

_____ *Let's do this* _____

DATE COMPLETED _____ LOCATION _____
SOLO / WITH _____
THE STORY _____
_____
_____
_____
_____
_____

THE BEST PART _____
_____
_____

WHAT I LEARNED _____
_____
_____

56

I WANT TO DO THIS BECAUSE _____
_____

TO MAKE THIS HAPPEN I NEED TO _____
_____

_____ *Let's do this* _____

DATE COMPLETED _____ LOCATION _____
SOLO / WITH _____
THE STORY _____
_____
_____
_____
_____
_____
_____

THE BEST PART _____
_____
_____

WHAT I LEARNED _____
_____
_____
_____

57

I WANT TO DO THIS BECAUSE _____

_____

TO MAKE THIS HAPPEN I NEED TO _____

_____

_____ *Let's do this* _____

DATE COMPLETED _____ LOCATION _____

SOLO / WITH _____

THE STORY _____

_____

_____

_____

_____

_____

_____

THE BEST PART _____

_____

_____

WHAT I LEARNED _____

_____

_____

58

_____

I WANT TO DO THIS BECAUSE _____
_____

TO MAKE THIS HAPPEN I NEED TO _____
_____

_____ *Let's do this* _____

DATE COMPLETED _____ LOCATION _____
SOLO / WITH _____
THE STORY _____
_____
_____
_____
_____
_____
_____

THE BEST PART _____
_____
_____

WHAT I LEARNED _____
_____
_____
_____

59

I WANT TO DO THIS BECAUSE _____

_____

TO MAKE THIS HAPPEN I NEED TO _____

_____

_____ *Let's do this* _____

DATE COMPLETED _____ LOCATION _____

SOLO / WITH _____

THE STORY_____

_____

_____

_____

_____

_____

THE BEST PART_____

_____

_____

WHAT I LEARNED_____

_____

_____

_____

60

_____

I WANT TO DO THIS BECAUSE _____

_____

TO MAKE THIS HAPPEN I NEED TO _____

_____

_____ *Let's do this* _____

DATE COMPLETED _____ LOCATION _____

SOLO / WITH _____

THE STORY _____

_____

_____

_____

_____

_____

THE BEST PART _____

_____

_____

WHAT I LEARNED _____

_____

_____

_____

61

I WANT TO DO THIS BECAUSE _____
_____

TO MAKE THIS HAPPEN I NEED TO_____
_____

_____ *Let's do this* _____

DATE COMPLETED _____ LOCATION _____
SOLO / WITH _____
THE STORY_____
_____
_____
_____
_____
_____
_____

THE BEST PART _____
_____
_____

WHAT I LEARNED_____
_____
_____
_____

62

I WANT TO DO THIS BECAUSE _____

_____

TO MAKE THIS HAPPEN I NEED TO _____

_____

_____ *Let's do this* _____

DATE COMPLETED _____ LOCATION _____

SOLO / WITH _____

THE STORY _____

_____

_____

_____

_____

_____

_____

THE BEST PART _____

_____

_____

WHAT I LEARNED _____

_____

_____

_____

63 _____

_____

I WANT TO DO THIS BECAUSE _____

_____

TO MAKE THIS HAPPEN I NEED TO _____

_____

_____ *Let's do this* _____

DATE COMPLETED _____ LOCATION _____

SOLO / WITH _____

THE STORY _____

_____

_____

_____

_____

_____

_____

THE BEST PART _____

_____

_____

WHAT I LEARNED _____

_____

_____

64

I WANT TO DO THIS BECAUSE _____

_____

TO MAKE THIS HAPPEN I NEED TO_____

_____

_____ *Let's do this* _____

DATE COMPLETED _____ LOCATION _____

SOLO / WITH _____

THE STORY_____

_____

_____

_____

_____

_____

_____

THE BEST PART_____

_____

_____

_____

WHAT I LEARNED_____

_____

_____

65 _____
_____

I WANT TO DO THIS BECAUSE _____
_____

TO MAKE THIS HAPPEN I NEED TO _____
_____

_____ *Let's do this* _____

DATE COMPLETED _____ LOCATION _____
SOLO / WITH _____
THE STORY _____
_____
_____
_____
_____
_____

THE BEST PART _____
_____
_____

WHAT I LEARNED _____
_____
_____

66

I WANT TO DO THIS BECAUSE _____

_____

TO MAKE THIS HAPPEN I NEED TO _____

_____

_____ *Let's do this* _____

DATE COMPLETED _____ LOCATION _____

SOLO / WITH _____

THE STORY_____

_____

_____

_____

_____

_____

THE BEST PART_____

_____

_____

WHAT I LEARNED_____

_____

_____

_____

67 _____
_____

I WANT TO DO THIS BECAUSE _____
_____

TO MAKE THIS HAPPEN I NEED TO _____
_____

_____ *Let's do this* _____

DATE COMPLETED _____ LOCATION _____
SOLO / WITH _____
THE STORY _____
_____
_____
_____
_____
_____
_____

THE BEST PART _____
_____
_____

WHAT I LEARNED _____
_____
_____
_____

68

_____

_____

I WANT TO DO THIS BECAUSE _____

_____

TO MAKE THIS HAPPEN I NEED TO _____

_____

_____ *Let's do this* _____

DATE COMPLETED _____ LOCATION _____

SOLO / WITH _____

THE STORY _____

_____

_____

_____

_____

_____

_____

THE BEST PART _____

_____

_____

WHAT I LEARNED _____

_____

_____

_____

69 _____
_____

I WANT TO DO THIS BECAUSE _____
_____

TO MAKE THIS HAPPEN I NEED TO _____
_____

_____ *Let's do this* _____

DATE COMPLETED _____ LOCATION _____
SOLO / WITH _____
THE STORY _____
_____
_____
_____
_____
_____
_____

THE BEST PART _____
_____
_____

WHAT I LEARNED _____
_____
_____
_____

70

I WANT TO DO THIS BECAUSE _____

_____

TO MAKE THIS HAPPEN I NEED TO _____

_____

_____ *Let's do this* _____

DATE COMPLETED _____ LOCATION _____

SOLO / WITH _____

THE STORY _____

_____

_____

_____

_____

_____

THE BEST PART _____

_____

_____

_____

WHAT I LEARNED _____

_____

_____

_____

71 _____

I WANT TO DO THIS BECAUSE _____

_____

TO MAKE THIS HAPPEN I NEED TO _____

_____

_____ *Let's do this* _____

DATE COMPLETED _____ LOCATION _____

SOLO / WITH _____

THE STORY _____

_____

_____

_____

_____

_____

THE BEST PART _____

_____

_____

WHAT I LEARNED _____

_____

_____

72

_____

_____

I WANT TO DO THIS BECAUSE _____
_____

TO MAKE THIS HAPPEN I NEED TO _____
_____

_____ *Let's do this* _____

DATE COMPLETED _____ LOCATION _____
SOLO / WITH _____
THE STORY _____
_____
_____
_____
_____
_____
_____

THE BEST PART _____
_____
_____
_____

WHAT I LEARNED _____
_____
_____
_____

73

I WANT TO DO THIS BECAUSE _____
_____

TO MAKE THIS HAPPEN I NEED TO _____
_____

Let's do this _____

DATE COMPLETED _____ LOCATION _____
SOLO / WITH _____
THE STORY _____
_____
_____
_____
_____
_____

THE BEST PART _____
_____
_____

WHAT I LEARNED _____
_____
_____

74

I WANT TO DO THIS BECAUSE _____

_____

TO MAKE THIS HAPPEN I NEED TO _____

_____

_____ *Let's do this* _____

DATE COMPLETED _____ LOCATION _____

SOLO / WITH _____

THE STORY_____

_____

_____

_____

_____

_____

_____

THE BEST PART_____

_____

_____

_____

WHAT I LEARNED_____

_____

_____

_____

75 _____
_____

I WANT TO DO THIS BECAUSE _____
_____

TO MAKE THIS HAPPEN I NEED TO _____
_____

_____ Let's do this _____

DATE COMPLETED _____ LOCATION _____
SOLO / WITH _____
THE STORY _____
_____
_____
_____
_____
_____

THE BEST PART _____
_____
_____

WHAT I LEARNED _____
_____
_____

76

I WANT TO DO THIS BECAUSE _____

_____

TO MAKE THIS HAPPEN I NEED TO _____

_____

_____ *Let's do this* _____

DATE COMPLETED _____ LOCATION _____

SOLO / WITH _____

THE STORY _____

_____

_____

_____

_____

_____

_____

THE BEST PART _____

_____

_____

WHAT I LEARNED _____

_____

_____

_____

77 _____

_____

I WANT TO DO THIS BECAUSE _____

_____

TO MAKE THIS HAPPEN I NEED TO _____

_____

_____ Let's do this _____

DATE COMPLETED _____ LOCATION _____

SOLO / WITH _____

THE STORY _____

_____

_____

_____

_____

_____

THE BEST PART _____

_____

_____

WHAT I LEARNED _____

_____

_____

_____

78

_____

_____

I WANT TO DO THIS BECAUSE _____

_____

TO MAKE THIS HAPPEN I NEED TO _____

_____

_____ *Let's do this* _____

DATE COMPLETED _____ LOCATION _____

SOLO / WITH _____

THE STORY _____

_____

_____

_____

_____

_____

_____

THE BEST PART _____

_____

_____

WHAT I LEARNED _____

_____

_____

_____

79

I WANT TO DO THIS BECAUSE _____

_____

TO MAKE THIS HAPPEN I NEED TO _____

_____

_____ *Let's do this* _____

DATE COMPLETED _____ LOCATION _____
SOLO / WITH _____
THE STORY_____

_____

_____

_____

_____

_____

THE BEST PART_____

_____

_____

WHAT I LEARNED_____

_____

_____

80

I WANT TO DO THIS BECAUSE _____

_____

TO MAKE THIS HAPPEN I NEED TO _____

_____

_____ *Let's do this* _____

DATE COMPLETED _____ LOCATION _____

SOLO / WITH _____

THE STORY _____

_____

_____

_____

_____

_____

_____

THE BEST PART _____

_____

_____

_____

WHAT I LEARNED _____

_____

_____

_____

81 _____
_____

I WANT TO DO THIS BECAUSE _____
_____

TO MAKE THIS HAPPEN I NEED TO _____
_____

_____ *Let's do this* _____

DATE COMPLETED _____ LOCATION _____

SOLO / WITH _____

THE STORY _____
_____
_____
_____
_____
_____
_____

THE BEST PART _____
_____
_____

WHAT I LEARNED _____
_____
_____
_____

_____ **82**
_____

I WANT TO DO THIS BECAUSE _____
_____

TO MAKE THIS HAPPEN I NEED TO _____
_____

_____ *Let's do this* _____

DATE COMPLETED _____ LOCATION _____
SOLO / WITH _____
THE STORY _____
_____
_____
_____
_____
_____
_____

THE BEST PART _____
_____
_____

WHAT I LEARNED _____
_____
_____

83 _____

I WANT TO DO THIS BECAUSE _____
_____

TO MAKE THIS HAPPEN I NEED TO _____
_____

_____ *Let's do this* _____

DATE COMPLETED _____ LOCATION _____
SOLO / WITH _____
THE STORY _____
_____
_____
_____
_____
_____
_____

THE BEST PART _____
_____
_____

WHAT I LEARNED _____
_____
_____

84

I WANT TO DO THIS BECAUSE _____
_____

TO MAKE THIS HAPPEN I NEED TO _____
_____

_____ *Let's do this* _____

DATE COMPLETED _____ LOCATION _____
SOLO / WITH _____
THE STORY _____
_____
_____
_____
_____
_____

THE BEST PART _____
_____
_____

WHAT I LEARNED _____
_____
_____
_____

85 _____

I WANT TO DO THIS BECAUSE _____
_____

TO MAKE THIS HAPPEN I NEED TO _____
_____

_____ *Let's do this* _____

DATE COMPLETED _____ LOCATION _____
SOLO / WITH _____
THE STORY _____
_____
_____
_____
_____
_____

THE BEST PART _____
_____
_____

WHAT I LEARNED _____
_____
_____
_____

86

_____

_____

I WANT TO DO THIS BECAUSE _____

_____

TO MAKE THIS HAPPEN I NEED TO _____

_____

_____ *Let's do this* _____

DATE COMPLETED _____ LOCATION _____

SOLO / WITH _____

THE STORY _____

_____

_____

_____

_____

_____

_____

THE BEST PART _____

_____

_____

_____

WHAT I LEARNED _____

_____

_____

_____

87

I WANT TO DO THIS BECAUSE _____

_____

TO MAKE THIS HAPPEN I NEED TO _____

_____

_____ Let's do this _____

DATE COMPLETED _____ LOCATION _____

SOLO / WITH _____

THE STORY _____

_____

_____

_____

_____

_____

_____

THE BEST PART _____

_____

_____

WHAT I LEARNED _____

_____

_____

88

I WANT TO DO THIS BECAUSE _____
_____

TO MAKE THIS HAPPEN I NEED TO _____
_____

_____ *Let's do this* _____

DATE COMPLETED _____ LOCATION _____
SOLO / WITH _____
THE STORY _____
_____
_____
_____
_____
_____
_____

THE BEST PART _____
_____
_____

WHAT I LEARNED _____
_____
_____
_____

89

I WANT TO DO THIS BECAUSE _____

_____

TO MAKE THIS HAPPEN I NEED TO _____

_____

_____ *Let's do this* _____

DATE COMPLETED _____ LOCATION _____

SOLO / WITH _____

THE STORY_____

_____

_____

_____

_____

_____

THE BEST PART_____

_____

_____

WHAT I LEARNED_____

_____

_____

_____

90

_____

_____

I WANT TO DO THIS BECAUSE _____

_____

TO MAKE THIS HAPPEN I NEED TO_____

_____

_____ *Let's do this* _____

DATE COMPLETED _____ LOCATION _____
SOLO / WITH _____
THE STORY_____

_____

_____

_____

_____

_____

_____

THE BEST PART_____

_____

_____

WHAT I LEARNED_____

_____

_____

91

I WANT TO DO THIS BECAUSE _____

_____

TO MAKE THIS HAPPEN I NEED TO _____

_____

_____ *Let's do this* _____

DATE COMPLETED _____ LOCATION _____
SOLO / WITH _____
THE STORY_____

_____

_____

_____

_____

_____

THE BEST PART_____

_____

_____

WHAT I LEARNED_____

_____

_____

_____

92

I WANT TO DO THIS BECAUSE _____

_____

TO MAKE THIS HAPPEN I NEED TO_____

_____

_____ *Let's do this* _____

DATE COMPLETED _____ LOCATION _____

SOLO / WITH _____

THE STORY_____

_____

_____

_____

_____

_____

_____

THE BEST PART_____

_____

_____

_____

WHAT I LEARNED_____

_____

_____

_____

93

I WANT TO DO THIS BECAUSE _____

_____

TO MAKE THIS HAPPEN I NEED TO _____

_____

_____ *Let's do this* _____

DATE COMPLETED _____ LOCATION _____

SOLO / WITH _____

THE STORY_____

_____

_____

_____

_____

_____

_____

THE BEST PART _____

_____

_____

WHAT I LEARNED_____

_____

_____

_____

94

I WANT TO DO THIS BECAUSE _____

_____

TO MAKE THIS HAPPEN I NEED TO_____

_____

_____ *Let's do this* _____

DATE COMPLETED _____ LOCATION _____

SOLO / WITH _____

THE STORY_____

_____

_____

_____

_____

_____

_____

THE BEST PART_____

_____

_____

_____

WHAT I LEARNED_____

_____

_____

_____

95 _____

_____

I WANT TO DO THIS BECAUSE _____

_____

TO MAKE THIS HAPPEN I NEED TO _____

_____

_____ *Let's do this* _____

DATE COMPLETED _____ LOCATION _____

SOLO / WITH _____

THE STORY _____

_____

_____

_____

_____

_____

_____

THE BEST PART _____

_____

_____

_____

WHAT I LEARNED _____

_____

_____

_____

96

_____

I WANT TO DO THIS BECAUSE _____
_____

TO MAKE THIS HAPPEN I NEED TO _____
_____

_____ *Let's do this* _____

DATE COMPLETED _____ LOCATION _____
SOLO / WITH _____
THE STORY _____
_____
_____
_____
_____
_____

THE BEST PART _____
_____
_____
_____

WHAT I LEARNED _____
_____
_____
_____

97 _____

_____

I WANT TO DO THIS BECAUSE _____

_____

TO MAKE THIS HAPPEN I NEED TO _____

_____

_____ *Let's do this* _____

DATE COMPLETED _____ LOCATION _____

SOLO / WITH _____

THE STORY _____

_____

_____

_____

_____

_____

THE BEST PART _____

_____

_____

WHAT I LEARNED _____

_____

_____

98

I WANT TO DO THIS BECAUSE _____

_____

TO MAKE THIS HAPPEN I NEED TO_____

_____

_____ *Let's do this* _____

DATE COMPLETED _____ LOCATION _____

SOLO / WITH _____

THE STORY_____

_____

_____

_____

_____

_____

_____

THE BEST PART_____

_____

_____

WHAT I LEARNED_____

_____

_____

_____

99 _____
_____

I WANT TO DO THIS BECAUSE _____
_____

TO MAKE THIS HAPPEN I NEED TO _____
_____

_____ *Let's do this* _____

DATE COMPLETED _____ LOCATION _____
SOLO / WITH _____
THE STORY _____
_____
_____
_____
_____
_____
_____

THE BEST PART _____
_____
_____

WHAT I LEARNED _____
_____
_____
_____

100

_____

I WANT TO DO THIS BECAUSE _____

TO MAKE THIS HAPPEN I NEED TO _____

Let's do this _____

DATE COMPLETED _____ LOCATION _____

SOLO / WITH _____

THE STORY _____

_____

_____

_____

_____

_____

THE BEST PART _____

_____

_____

WHAT I LEARNED _____

_____

_____

26587698R00059

Printed in Great Britain
by Amazon